Original title:
Nebula Narratives

Copyright © 2025 Creative Arts Management OÜ
All rights reserved.

Author: Julian Montgomery
ISBN HARDBACK: 978-1-80567-759-8
ISBN PAPERBACK: 978-1-80567-880-9

Astral Adventures

In spaceships shaped like cheese,
We zoom past stars with lots of ease.
Aliens in socks, they dance and sway,
   Turning our tour into a ballet.

With cosmic pies and fizzy drinks,
We chat with black holes, share our winks.
Space cats play with swirling dust,
   It's a hilarious cosmic bust!

The Fabric of Cosmic Wonder

Stars are knitted with silver thread,
Comets weave tales while half asleep in bed.
Galaxies unfold like quilts so grand,
While Pluto throws a mooncake stand.

Planets gossip about their mates,
Jupiter boasts on waving plates.
Saturn flips pancakes on its rings,
In this cosmic realm, everybody sings!

The Soundtrack of Distant Worlds

In the void, a quirky tune,
Played by a squirrel who hums to the moon.
Mars beats drums made of conch shells,
Jupiter giggles, as laughter swells.

Neptune's flute made of frozen tears,
Echoes through space, charms spacecraft peers.
Meanwhile, a trumpet from the sun,
Makes it clear, this party's begun!

Echoes in the Starlight

Whispers of stardust fill the night,
With cheeky comets, a playful sight.
Laughter ricochets off cosmic glass,
As meteors dance, gliding past.

Wormholes giggle, twisting tight,
While galaxies waltz in dazzling light.
Echos of laughter floating around,
In this stellar spree, joy is found!

The Infinity of Starry Songs

In the cosmos, cats wear hats,
Singing to stars and fluffy rats.
They juggle comets, sip sweet tea,
While space whales dance, wild and free.

Planets prance in glittery shoes,
Dancing to tunes from cosmic blues.
Aliens chuckle, swap funny jokes,
As meteor showers rain down folks.

Every twinkling star's a bright smile,
Tickling the void, traveling in style.
Galactic giggles echo through light,
As night prepares for a cosmic flight.

So, in the vast and shimmering night,
Join the laughter, embrace the light!
For in this tale of starry glee,
The universe sings eternally.

Dreaming in the Cosmos

In dreams, I float on candy clouds,
With chocolate stars, I shout out loud.
Marshmallow moons in a strawberry sky,
Where jellybeans spin and sing nearby.

Gravity giggles as I tumble down,
Flipping and flopping, no need to frown.
Comets whizz by wearing big sunglasses,
While dancing ducks form silly masses.

Planets twirl, wearing funky hats,
Cosmic conga with astrobot chats.
Slipping on stardust, spinning with glee,
The universe tickles, just wait and see.

Up here, dreams are bright, laughter flows,
In galactic gardens where humor grows.
So join the fun, take a joyful ride,
In a cosmic dream where giggles collide.

Whispers of Cosmic Dreams

Stars whisper secrets with a grin,
Telling tales of where they've been.
A snail in space with a shell of cheese,
Slides by, making the universe tease.

Planets giggle, bounce in delight,
As comets parade in the shimmering light.
A mouse on Mars makes a cheesy show,
Dancing with craters, stealing the glow.

Black holes burp, creating a fuss,
A cosmic ruckus, just for us.
While moonbeams tickle sleeping stars,
In endless laughter, ignoring the scars.

So listen close to the cosmic hum,
Where funny dreams and giggles come.
In this starlit tale, the chuckles beam,
As we float away in a cosmic dream.

Starlight Silhouettes

In starlight, shadows play peek-a-boo,
Dancing with comets that travel askew.
Nebulous giggles round every bend,
As constellations wink and transcend.

The moon acts silly, with pranks up its sleeve,
While stardust sparkles, just to deceive.
Aliens play hopscotch on Saturn's rings,
Making a racket as the universe sings.

Galaxies twist, forming funny shapes,
While space cows float in astronaut capes.
With a whoosh and a whirl, the cosmos spins,
In a merry dance where every joke wins.

So take a step in this playful night,
Join in the fun, feel the delight.
For under this canopy of twinkling jet,
Life's a grand stage, no need for regret.

Pulsars and Poets

In the cosmos, poets spin,
Twirling rhymes, let the fun begin.
With pulsars blinking in wacky style,
They scribble sonnets that make us smile.

Stars giggle as they twinklingly dance,
While poets often forget their pants.
In cosmic cafes, they sip stardust tea,
Writing silly verses, all carefree.

Galaxies swirl like a cosmic stew,
With verses of laughter, the void's debut.
A rhyme's a joke that's floated in space,
With meteors laughing, it's quite the race.

So grab your quill and a comet's tail,
Join the poets on their vibrant trail.
In this universe, humor's the key,
Where laughter's the spark of eternity.

Celestial Rhapsody

Planets sing in major key,
As comets crash like a messy spree.
Asteroids tumble, a clumsy ballet,
In this cosmic romp, we frolic and play.

Saturn's rings jingle, what a sight,
Dancing round the sun, oh what a bite!
With cosmic hiccups, the orbits align,
Even black holes know how to unwind.

Stars throw parties with a wink and a nod,
While stardust confetti rains down on the odd.
A giggle erupts from a distant quasar,
As the universe roars with laughter afar.

Our galactic jesters are bold and bright,
Chasing infinity in the dark of night.
With cosmic punchlines spun on a whim,
The great dance of humor, let's all join in!

The Stardust Diary

In the dusty vaults of the Milky Way,
A poet scribbles down what stars say.
With a wink, he writes about a space cat,
Whose UFO swirls in a cosmic chat.

Planets gossip, they tilt and tease,
Jupiter's jokes bring the cosmos to freeze.
Venus pretends to be shy and coy,
While Martian laughter echoes with joy.

The poet spills ink that twinkles and glows,
Words jump around in a twirly prose.
As he pens down tales of aliens' fun,
His diary sparkles like a supernova run.

So flip through pages of this stellar lore,
With witticisms from the universe's core.
For in this diary of humor and light,
We find our joy in the cosmic night.

Whispers in the Cosmic Wind

In cosmic breezes, whispers abound,
With alien giggles, the void's lively sound.
Stars share secrets with a twinkle and grin,
While comets make mischief, let the fun begin.

Galactic wind carries fables and tales,
Of laughter on Mars and interstellar gales.
Black holes chuckle at the planets' plight,
Holding their jokes in the depths of night.

Through the cosmos, puns travel fast,
Like shooting stars, they'll never last.
But oh what joy in their fleeting spree,
As laughter echoes in eternity.

Join the whispers, let your giggles soar,
In a universe vast, there's always more.
For in friendly jest, we find our way,
In the cosmic wind, forever we'll play.

Tales from the Celestial Canvas

In a galaxy far, far away,
Tiny aliens loved to play.
They painted stars with jellybeans,
And giggled at their funny schemes.

Planets danced in cosmic cheer,
Wobbling, spinning without fear.
They'd throw a ball made of stardust,
And share light-years' worth of trust.

Comets zipped with silly grins,
They reveled in their candy wins.
Chasing meteors with glee,
Creating chaos for all to see.

Yet when the sun began to set,
They'd laugh about their cosmic debt.
For every star that they had painted,
Their own backsides were quite feinted!

Lightyears of Lamentation

Lightyears passed with loads of fuss,
Asteroids made quite the ruckus.
A space cow lost its favorite shoe,
Crying stars that glistened blue!

In the void, a rabbit sighed,
From stardust dreams, it never hides.
"Why must I hop through endless night?"
It wished for cake, oh what a sight!

A wormhole opened with a yawn,
Sucked in dreams at the break of dawn.
With each swirl, a giggle ran,
For even space has its own plan!

Comets laughed, sharing sweet tales,
Of cosmic wind and vibrant gales.
Lightyears won't stop this fun parade,
For in this cosmic mess, we're made!

Veils of Celestial Mystery

Behind the veil where stars do peek,
Galactic whispers do unique speak.
'Why is gravity such a bore?'
Wondrous worlds ponder evermore.

A singing planet strewn with charms,
Beamed hugs wrapped in cosmic arms.
It giggled when the moons would tease,
"I'm the best! Oh, can't you see?"

A black hole danced the tango true,
"Don't pull me in, oh please don't do!"
With flailing arms and swirling grace,
It twirled in pure, hilarious space!

Yet as the cosmos spun around,
A riddle formed with silly sound.
Does laughter echo through the night?
Oh yes, the stars are out of sight!

Through the Eyes of Distant Stars

Stars peered down with winking eyes,
Observing life with sweet surprise.
A kid on Earth slipped on a shoe,
And sent his pet cat flying too!

From afar, a star exclaimed,
"Those Earthlings really are quite game!"
While meteors raced past with flair,
"Let's join the fun, if we dare!"

Saturn's rings spun tales of woe,
How many lost their favorite show?
"Just press rewind!" one boldly cried,
"Let's binge on laughs, we cannot hide!"

And in the end, with twinkling glee,
The universe shared its decree.
To laugh, to play, to freely roam,
In every heart, the stars find home!

Beyond the Celestial Veil

Among the stars, I lost my keys,
Floating near a pair of knees.
Galaxies giggle, they wink and beam,
Space is funny; it's all a dream.

Asteroids dance in twirls of grace,
In this vast and silly place.
Planets play hide and seek from light,
While comets argue about their flight.

Aliens toss their hats so high,
They miss the catch and wave goodbye.
With cosmic jokes that never fade,
Laughter fills this grand parade.

So join the fun outside the Earth,
Let stardust tickle your mirth.
In this realm where starlight pranks,
We'll chuckle while the universe spans.

One Thousand Colors of the Milky Way

Stars spilled paint upon the sky,
One green moon began to cry.
Purple planets with hats askew,
Asked the sun if it laughed too.

A comet tripped, a glitter fall,
Came crashing down—ouch! Not small!
The cosmos chuckles, a playful tease,
While planets dance in cosmic breeze.

Rainbow aliens slap high fives,
Wobbling on their rubbery lives.
Fifty shades of cosmic glee,
In space, there's endless comedy.

So grab your brush, and paint your dreams,
Let colors burst in giggling streams.
For in the vast, bright twisted play,
Laughter's hue lights up the way.

The Echo of Cosmic Incantations

In the void, whispers collide,
Spooky giggles, space is wide.
Wizards float, poorly dressed,
Casting spells with quirky zest.

A black hole yawns, oh what a sight,
Sucking up the snacks at night.
Cosmic cats say "meow" so bright,
Chasing shadows in the starlight.

With each incantation tossed,
Galactic giggles, never lost.
Gravity grumbles, "I'm not a clown!"
But the universe wears a funny gown.

So gather 'round, let's cast some fun,
In this cosmic playground run.
Echoes ring across the dark,
Take a chance; let's leave a mark!

Constellation Confessions

Orion told a tale so bright,
Of missing pants during the night.
A starry giggle, a twinkling tease,
He blushed and chuckled, "Oh, please!"

The Dippers dipped into the stew,
Sipped the Milky way—who knew?
While Cassiopeia sang a tune,
About a cat that loved the moon.

"Big dipper, small dipper, where's the snack?"
They jostled about, then grabbed a pack.
And Venus couldn't help but grin,
As space shenanigans would begin.

So listen closely to the night,
The stars are giddy, pure delight.
Their secrets shared on cosmic wings,
In confessions, laughter sings.

The Tapestry of the Universe

A giant quilt of stars above,
Sewed by cosmic hands that shove,
Each thread a tale, each patch a joke,
How'd they fit it? With sheer smoke!

Planets collide, they laugh and spin,
Why don't they ever let me in?
I knock on Mars, but it just shrugs,
Says it's busy, and gives me bugs!

The moons waltz in a dance-up high,
While comets crack up, oh my, oh my!
"Can we take selfies?" they often plead,
But gravity's strict, leaves them in need.

In the cosmic diner, stars throw fries,
They giggle and glow with light in their eyes,
Order a black hole, it's quite the trick,
It swallows your drink—oh, isn't space slick?

Celestial Poetry

A shooting star zipped through the night,
Spilling secrets of flight and fright.
"Did you hear that? The Milky Way's tales!
One's about cows and intergalactic trails!"

Saturn's rings are just party hats,
Worn by aliens and their chatty cats.
They spill their drinks in cosmic delight,
While Earthlings debate if Pluto's still bright.

Jupiter's storms are just wild dance moves,
Twisting and turning, oh how it grooves!
"Hold my drink!" cries an astronaut bold,
As space itself laughs, both young and old.

Passing black holes sell popcorn and dreams,
Their laughter echoes, split at the seams.
Cosmic rhymes in the vastness unfurl,
Making giggles explode in this strange swirl!

Light Years to Remember

In light years gone, I lost my sock,
Floating somewhere near the cosmic rock.
Aliens snicker, 'A fashion faux pas!'
"Can't you see? It's all just for Jaws!"

Star dust tastes like old pizza crust,
While traveling time, you might combust.
"Hey, Earthling, got change for a dime?"
"Not in space, buddy, just lost track of time!"

Supernova parties are all the rage,
Where stars break out, free from a cage.
Shooting star DJs spin it right,
While asteroids slam—what a chaotic night!

A wormhole whispers, "Hey, wanna race?"
"Sure," I say, "But keep up that pace!"
Off we dart, we laugh and scream,
Space is weird—oh, what a dream!

Space Between Heartbeats

In the crevice of space, time takes a break,
Electrons giggle, "Make no mistake!"
A heartbeat's pause gives stars a chance,
To twirl and whirl in a quirky dance.

Constellations swap stories like shoes,
"Whose turn is it now for the blues?"
As meteors crash with mugs of hot tea,
Orbiting chaos, what a sight to see!

Void of silence, whispers abound,
Aliens subtly make goofy sounds.
A comet rolls in with a wink and a cheer,
"Join our parade, it's the best time of year!"

Galaxies chuckle till dark turns to light,
In this cosmic prank of sheer delight.
So let's dance 'neath the stars, find laughter so sweet,
In the space between heartbeats, let joy be our beat!

Celestial Threads

In the cosmos where stars do grin,
A comet tripped on its own tail fin.
With a wink, it spun around the bend,
Saying, "Who knew space could be a friend?"

Galaxies dance like they just don't care,
A black hole snickered, "Not my hair!"
Planets play hide and seek with delight,
While meteors streak and spark through the night.

Echoes of the Infinite

In vast voids where echoes play,
Asteroids argue on the Milky Way.
"You're not as shiny as you think you are!"
"Oh yeah? Just ask my buddy, the star!"

Jupiter's big but doesn't see,
His moons gossip, "Is he just vanity?"
The rings of Saturn giggle with glee,
While Venus snorts coffee, "Look at me!"

Stardust Journeys

A spaceship sneezed, it went 'ACHOO!'
Leaving trails of stardust in a hula-hoop.
Aliens chuckled, "What's wrong with that?"
While cosmic cats purred, curled up on a mat.

Rockets tried dancing, a wobbly jig,
But engines went pop, oh what a dig!
The stars took bets on who'd fall down,
While black holes rolled laughing, wearing a crown.

Luminary Tales

A sunbeam whispered a secret word,
While moons spread tales just as absurd.
"Did you hear? It's raining light!"
Stars donned umbrellas, what a sight!

Supernovas threw confetti in space,
While shooting stars battled in a race.
Galactic giggles echoed through night,
As asteroids danced in sheer delight.

Portraits of Time and Space

In the jar of the cosmos, they collect the past,
Aliens play poker, the stakes are vast.
Stars waltz through the void, wearing shades of bright,
While asteroids argue over who's faster in flight.

Time falsely claims it's a linear race,
While comets just laugh, like it's all a big space.
Planets take selfies with moons in the frame,
And the sun beams down, shouting, "Who's got the fame?"

In black holes, they find a great twist of fate,
Where lost socks and puzzles do gather and wait.
Quasars hold parties, with light years on mead,
And the cosmos whispers, "Do you want a good deed?"

So here is a story of time, light, and cheer,
Where each cosmic creature has something to share.
Amongst the vast wonders, in absolute grace,
You'll find jokes and laughter in time and in space.

Light from Cosmic Shores

On the beach of the cosmos, waves shimmer and glow,
Starfish tell tales that only they know.
The moon's having cocktails with stars in a line,
While space crabs dig holes in their crystalline brine.

A comet's a surfer, just catching a ride,
While black holes make whirlpools for fun in the tide.
Galactic winds breeze, like a soft summer breeze,
While aliens chuckle, gossiping with ease.

Jellyfish cosmos dance in colors so bright,
Planetary fish swim with shimmering light.
With meteor showers, they laugh and they play,
Crafting jokes out of stardust, come what may.

And so from the shores of this vast cosmic sea,
Where laughter rings out, wild and carefree.
You'll learn that the universe, far and near,
Is a playground of light, where joy should appear.

Cosmic Blossoms

In the garden of stars, flowers bloom every night,
With petals of stardust, oh what a sight!
Galaxies giggle as they spin in a twirl,
While meteors race, like they're late for a whirl.

Nebulae stretch, posing for selfies so grand,
While planets discuss how to start a rock band.
Asteroids carve sculptures, a cosmic display,
And gravity wonders, "Will I get in the way?"

In the springs of dark matter, life has its quirks,
With robots who paint and play cosmic jerks.
They blow bubbles of light, as they float in the void,
Crafting laughter from chaos, joyfully deployed.

So venture, dear stargazer, on this laughter quest,
Where blossoms of light make the universe best.
With each twinkle and star, there's a giggle or two,
In the garden of wonders, waiting just for you.

Songs of Distant Galaxies

From the edge of the cosmos, tunes start to hum,
While pulsars play spoons, oh what a strum!
Singing planets croon softly, under the night,
While dark matter dances, what a curious sight.

Each galaxy's laughter is music to hear,
As comets play trumpets, they spread cosmic cheer.
Supernovae shout from the depths of their song,
Telling tales of the cosmos, where we all belong.

In the choir of starlight, the universe sways,
With notes of creation that echo for days.
So grab a friend meteor, and join in the fun,
Let's sing out together, 'til we're all done.

For the songs of the cosmos are playful and bright,
Inviting all beings to dance in the light.
So here's to the melodies that lead us to roam,
In the vast, twinkling garden, we all call home.

Harmonics of the Heavens

In the sky where stars align,
Comets dance and swirl in line.
Planets giggle, moons all wink,
Even black holes pause to think.

Cosmic chords that twist and bend,
Singing tales of space to send.
A chorus of the weird and bright,
Galactic jokes take off in flight.

The sun beams down with jokes to share,
While asteroids throw pies in air.
Gravity can't hold back the fun,
In this place where we've just begun.

So come along, join in the cheer,
Where laughter echoes—oh so near.
Across the stars, let spirits soar,
In the cosmos, we all want more.

Interstellar Stories

Once a star fell with a thud,
Landed in a spacey mud.
"Now I'm stuck!" it started to pout,
Until a friend said, "Let's dance about!"

Planets played a game of tag,
Jupiter yelled, "You're such a brag!"
Uranus laughed, "Well, I'm quite round,"
As meteors zipped and spun around.

Galaxies tugging at old tales,
Of martian cows and lunar whales.
Comets bring snacks to share and munch,
A cosmic picnic, join the lunch!

A rocket sneezed, who'd have guessed?
Shooting stars laughed, "We're truly blessed!"
In this story, all's a delight,
In the vastness, fun takes flight.

The Language of Starshine

Flashbulbs blink like tiny eyes,
Sending winks across the skies.
Stars have secrets, oh so bright,
Whispering jokes with all their might.

Mars mailed Venus a cheeky note,
Said, "I'm red and you're the dope!"
Laughter rippling through the void,
While asteroids just felt annoyed.

Meteor showers pouring down,
While aliens danced in a gown.
They grooved to beats from far-off suns,
Telling tales of space-bound runs.

Each twinkle bursts with glee and cheer,
Messages of fun, all crystal clear.
So gather 'round this cosmic glee,
In the language of light, we are free.

Echoing Across the Cosmos

Echoes bounce through cosmic halls,
Laughter rings as gravity calls.
Nebulas brim with clownish glee,
Shooting stars join in with a key.

Saturn's rings, a juggling show,
With moons as acrobats, don't you know?
"Watch me spin, catch this gaze!"
As planets chuckle through the haze.

Galactic giggles stack and grow,
Creating ripples, a comic flow.
A black hole jokes, "I'm the life of this,"
While stardust flutters in cosmic bliss.

Together we hum a joyful tune,
Dancing through the vastness of June.
So let us laugh, let us play,
In the cosmos, where fun finds a way.

Constellation Chronicles

In a cosmic café, stars sip tea,
The Milky Way's a pastry shop, you'll see.
Saturn's rings serve as silver platters,
While comets gossip, oh, the chitchat matters.

Uranus rolls in, what a clumsy sight,
Tripping on stardust, oh what a fright!
Mars jokes with Venus, their laughter's loud,
Planetary parties attract quite a crowd.

Galactic squirrels chase asteroids for fun,
Playing hide and seek with the sun.
Black holes hoot, "We swallow all snacks!",
Confetti from supernovae fills the cracks.

So when you gaze at the sky so bright,
Remember the antics of stars at night.
Each twinkle a wink, a cosmic jest,
In the great universe, laughter's the best!

Mysteries of the Void

In the vastness, floating ducks galore,
Quacking about mystery, who could ask for more?
They paddle through starlight, a silly parade,
With quarks and quirks in a cosmic charade.

A wormhole insists it's a travel agency,
Offering trips to worlds we've yet to see.
But every brochure is an awkward lie,
It's really just a place where lost socks sigh!

Asteroids are skaters, zipping past with glee,
Doing pirouettes, oh they're wild and free.
Meteor showers are just showers of joy,
Like kids with sparklers, oh what a ploy!

But don't be misled by the silent night,
For in the darkness, there's giggling, just right.
The mysteries unfold with a burst of glee,
In the void, where silliness runs wild and free!

Celestial Cartography

Drawing maps in space with buttered toast,
Every star is a crumb, for what we love most.
Chocolate milky rivers, let's sail away,
While jellybean comets dance and play.

Cartographers argue if Pluto fits in,
They argue so loud, they broke out in grin.
A star, with a pencil, giving them sass,
"More than a planet, I'm a cosmic mass!"

Elves in the ozone are plotting a show,
"We'll   start with stardust, then sprinkle in glow."
With bright balloons and confetti from skies,
They celebrate maps drawn with whimsical ties.

So if you're lost in the cosmic expanse,
Just follow the laughter, it's your best chance.
For in celestial charts, there's fun everywhere,
Just watch for the signs—take the ride, if you dare!

Fragments of a Starry Night

Under a sky full of glitter and gleam,
A moonbeam's got a riddle—it's quite the theme.
Stars play hide and seek, with silly grace,
While aliens giggle, just floating in space.

Teasing the Milky Way with popcorn so bright,
It spills on the cosmos, what a delicious sight!
Supernovae pop like confetti galore,
Leaving cosmic crumbs for the stardust store.

Shooting stars whiz by, calling "Catch me if you can!"
But shadowy planets just say, "No can!"
Each twinkle a whisper, "Join in on the fun,"
While comets flash by, with tail like a bun!

So when stargazing, let laughter take flight,
Join the starry party, it's an endless delight.
In every bright cluster, a chuckle awaits,
For fragments of night hold the universe's traits!

Astral Echoes Through Time

In a galaxy far, quite sublime,
Stars forgot to learn how to rhyme.
A comet sneezes with a flare,
Leaving stardust in the air.

Black holes dance, twirling with glee,
While astronauts sip their cosmic tea.
Planets bump, a party quite grand,
With Saturn in a polka-dot band.

Meteor showers bring drinks from afar,
Sipping moonlight, just like a star.
Aliens chuckle, they find it odd,
When earthlings think they're just a facade.

Time slips by on a whimsied ride,
While Jupiter takes the waltz in stride.
Galactic games of hide and seek,
With space as their playground, unique and meek.

Orbiting Whispers of Wonder

Planets gossip, what a great sight,
Mercury's quick, can't hold him tight.
Venus giggles, blushing so bright,
As Earth rolls her eyes, annoying at night.

Mars with his jokes, all red and round,
While Uranus swirls in laughable sound.
Neptune snickers, whispers of old,
"Hey Pluto, your status is cold!"

The Milky Way plays hide and seek,
While asteroids race, a fun little streak.
"Catch me!" they shout, what a ruckus they make,
As stars shine brightly, with no time to break.

Galaxies swirl with laughter so sweet,
Dancing through the dark, rhythmic beat.
In cosmic realms where dreams intertwine,
Orbiting whispers in a grand design.

The Symphony of Celestial Tales

The sun strums lightly on golden strings,
As planets hum and cosmic joy sings.
The moon conducts a show so divine,
While comets solo, leaving trails fine.

Saturn claps with its glowing rings,
While Mars beats drums, oh the joy it brings!
Jupiter booms like thunderous laughs,
Creating a symphony of cosmic gaffes.

Aliens join in with their party tune,
Dancing on meteors, under the moon.
"Let's wobble!" they yell, shaking their hue,
As starry notes blend in a celestial brew.

By starlight's glow, the universe sways,
As laughter echoes through infinite days.
In this concert of laughter and light,
Celestial tales sparkle through the night.

Fractured Light and Cosmic Echoes

Photons trip, then giggle and play,
As light beams bounce on a bright sunny day.
"Oops!" they proclaim, as they crash into time,
Fragmented sparkles, a chaotic rhyme.

Cosmic echoes rumble, tinged with delight,
As particles dance in the cool, starry night.
"Catch me!" shouts a wave, in a hurry to flee,
Creating a ruckus in the dark, oh so free.

Galaxies swirl, spinning out of control,
With dizzying motions, they put on a show.
"Oops, I bumped Mars!" the stellar winds tease,
As they zoom around with the greatest of ease.

Fractured light follows paths of its own,
While laughter erupts in celestial tone.
In the vastness of space, chaos takes flight,
With echoes of humor, shining so bright.

Lost in Celestial Translation

I asked a star what time it was,
It winked and said, "Just look around."
My watch got lost in space, it seems,
Now I'm late for galactic rounds.

The moon is full, but I misplaced,
My telescope in icy space.
Instead of stars, I see a raccoon,
Wearing a helmet, humming a tune.

Black holes ate my homework, quite,
They said it's too dense, out of sight.
I thought they'd give it just a pass,
But I'm now graded an 'intergalactic class.'

When comets dance, there's much to see,
A space jig and cosmic glee.
But lost in translation, I don't complain,
For laughter lights up the cosmic lane.

Memories Across Light Years

I sent a postcard to the sun,
Said, 'Hey there, it's hot, let's have fun!'
But all I got was a solar glare,
And now I'm stuck in a flaming chair.

Galaxies spin like spins of yarn,
Caught in a breeze of cosmic charm.
I'd write a book but what to say?
Each page a black hole, fading away.

They say time flies, but I'm unsure,
My clock just left for an alien tour.
With every tick, there's no turning back,
Just floating thoughts on a comet track.

Memories leak like stardust streams,
Filling my head with bizarre dreams.
I'll remember this spacey flight,
But lost the plot in the starry night.

Perspectives from the Cosmos

From Mars, I sent a selfie pic,
But the WiFi there is really sick.
All I got was a pixel mess,
And now I dress in space distress.

On Jupiter, the storms do brew,
But I stayed inside, forgot my shoe.
While spinning rings made a grand parade,
I sipped on space tea, unafraid.

Saturn winked with its icy gaze,
Said, 'Come party in my rings and haze!'
But lost my invitation halfway through,
Turns out a space whale's my plus-two.

Asteroids roll like bowling balls,
In this cosmos with bumpy calls.
With laughter echoing through the void,
Perspectives shift, humor deployed.

Starlit Songlines

I followed the song of a shooting star,
Hoping to find where wishes are.
It led me on a whimsical chase,
Through stardust trails and cosmic space.

The planets sing in offbeat rhymes,
While meteors dance to different chimes.
But I tripped over a wayward light,
And rolled on through the heavenly night.

Asteroids swoop like they own the place,
Cracking jokes with a close-knit grace.
While I giggle at their grand display,
Hopping on clouds, I bounce away.

In the end, I found my tune,
Whistled low with a dusk-lit moon.
Through starlit paths, I've come to see,
The fun in space is key for me.

Stories Written in Stardust

In the sky, a cat took flight,
Chasing comets in the night.
With a hat made from the moon,
He hummed a cosmic tune.

Stars giggled as they twinkled,
While planets danced and winkled.
Jupiter served green tea with zest,
While Saturn wore a polka dot vest.

A silly moonbeams' game they played,
As cosmic pranks were quickly laid.
Mars painted red with laughter's flair,
And Neptune joined with eccentric hair.

In this shimmering space delight,
Where stardust laughs burst the night.
Join the fun, let visions sway,
In stories spun from far away.

The Unseen Weavers of the Cosmos

A spider spins on a shooting star,
Weaving webs of dreams from afar.
With threads made from moonbeams bright,
She giggles in the gentle night.

Oh, the universe is quite a show,
With starry yarns that ebb and flow.
Galaxies dance with frolicsome cheer,
As comets giggle, drawing near.

Black holes whisper funny jokes,
And stardust tickles all the folks.
The cosmos twirls, a merry spin,
Where winks and blinks are woven in.

A tapestry of cosmic fun,
Where laughter rises with the sun.
In the dark, let mirth unfold,
With threads of laughter, bright and bold.

Celestial Reflections

Mirror, mirror, made of light,
Casting giggles into night.
Planets peek with silly grins,
As laughter in stardust spins.

Reflections beam from cosmic pools,
Where sneaky stars play by the rules.
A galaxy's wink, a playful nod,
In spirals of joy, how odd!

Comets chase the sun's bright rays,
While moonbeams join in playful plays.
A cluster of laughter, bright and bold,
In swirling colors, tales unfold.

Through the cosmos, hearts abound,
In light's embrace, pure joy is found.
Dance in shadows, cheer in sight,
As the universe tickles the night.

Light and Shadow in the Void

In the void, a shadow sneezed,
A starlight giggle, laughter teased.
With bright flickers bouncing high,
They played hide and seek in the sky.

The sun wore shades, oh what a sight,
Blocking rays in cheeky delight.
Planets played peek-a-boo all day,
As meteors zoomed, shouting "Hooray!"

Whispers of comets with tails so bright,
Tangled in laughter, pure cosmic light.
A jester in orbit spun around,
With cosmic jokes that knew no bound.

In the dance of shadow and gleam,
All the stars conspire and dream.
In the void, where laughter's loud,
join the fun, be merry, be proud!

Tales Adrift in the Galaxy

In a ship fueled by fizzy soda,
The captain wore socks and a toga.
Stars winked at his dance so grand,
He tickled the cosmos with rubber band.

Aliens laughed at a silly plight,
They ordered takeout from the moonlight.
Trading jokes across the great void,
Laughing 'till their galactic joy's deployed.

A comet sneezed, what a sight to behold,
Asteroids rolled, they were fifty years old.
Twinkling giggles filled the black space,
As laughter culminated in a swirling embrace.

Floating through space like a bounce on a trampoline,
They craved cosmic ice cream, the ultimate cuisine.
With flavors of starlight and quirks so bright,
Their bellies felt heavy with delight every night.

The Color of Silent Stars

Stars in pajamas, all comfy and tight,
Whispering colors in the still of the night.
One felt blue, the other was red,
They started a band from their cozy bed.

A purple star played the kazoo, oh so grand,
While green ones clapped, it was quite a band.
They sang about comets who lost their way,
And asteroids popping like popcorn in play.

While supernovas twinkled with glee,
A pastel rainbow brewed up some tea.
They laughed at the black holes, so moody and dark,
And tossed glitter flamingos, leaving their mark.

As colors swirled in a cosmic dance,
Even serious stars couldn't help but prance.
In the vast sky, the hues intertwined,
Creating a canvas, lovingly defined.

Stardust Reflections

In a mirror made of glistening space,
Stars check their hair as they pucker and brace.
One star complained of a bad hair day,
While meteors teased, 'Just let it sway!'

A cluster of stars wrote a diary at night,
Documenting who'd lost their starlight.
'Vegan space dust gave me a glow,' they said,
But taco tales filled them with dread.

Reflections glittered, a comical fray,
As lunars debated their style in a play.
'You should try polka dots!' said the moon,
While stardust chuckled a silly cartoon.

In the bright cosmos, giggles were shared,
Selfie snaps taken, no one was spared.
With glitter and laughter, the night was aglow,
In the mirror of dreams, stars put on a show.

Whispered Secrets of the Sky

In the quiet of night, the stars all conspire,
Whispers of gossip stretch far and higher.
'The sun's such a show-off, we'll give him a fright,'
They plotted in twinkles, so sly and light.

The clouds looked on, rolling their eyes,
While bats donned capes, taking to the skies.
'Let's play hide-and-seek with the Milky Way,'
They chuckled, as shadows began to sway.

Uranus blushed, caught in a tale,
As Pluto joined in, with his dog, named Gale.
They giggled and spun in a cosmic ballet,
Sharing secrets of worlds far away.

At dawn, they retreated, the laughter subsided,
As the sun peeked through, their giggles confided.
But the stars knew well, beneath the bright hue,
Their secrets would linger, shared just with the few.

Stardust Illusions

In the night sky, stars get confused,
They trip over clouds, feeling amused.
A comet sneezes, sending starlight,
While planets gossip, oh what a sight!

Saturn's rings dance in a swirl,
Jupiter's moons join in a twirl.
Aliens giggle, sipping space tea,
Making wishes on a shooting spree!

Asteroids chuckle as they play tag,
While black holes hum a cosmic rag.
Supernovae burst with a pop,
Leaving stardust trails that never stop!

Galaxies spin like tops in flight,
Creating chaos, pure delight.
With each twinkle, a joke is made,
In the vastness, hilarity won't fade!

Illuminated Verses

Bright stars wink with a cheeky cheer,
While space critters munch on cosmic beer.
The sun tries to tan on a moonlit beach,
But shadows laugh, 'It's too far to reach!'

Cosmic winds play a funky tune,
As meteorites dance in the light of the moon.
Aliens flip through their funny books,
While the Milky Way plays hide and seeks!

The Earth's garden grows flowers of light,
Watering them with starlit delight.
Earthworms moonwalk in glee, you see,
Telling fish jokes to the deep black sea!

Shooting stars zip with a whoosh and a dash,
Painting the sky in a glittery splash.
In laughter and light, the cosmos conspire,
With every twinkle, they dream and retire!

Beyond the Astral Plains

Cosmic cowboys ride stellar beams,
Rustling up starlight, chasing dreams.
Planets wear boots, spin in a line,
While the Milky Way serves up moonshine!

Galactic sheriffs chase runaway stars,
In spaceships racing past Venus and Mars.
With whoops and hollers, they join the fray,
Strange galaxies join the wild play!

Astroids in hats tip their brims,
While space whales sing at the universe's whims.
Black holes have parties with snacks in tow,
Warping the fun and stealing the show!

Cosmic critters laugh, sharing a jest,
In the silence of night, they party the best.
Beyond all limits, in laughter they soar,
In the cosmos, humor is never a bore!

Celestial Silences

In quiet voids where silence reigns,
Stars whisper secrets in glittering chains.
A quasar yawns, and the cosmos sighs,
While an old comet tells half-baked lies.

Space cats purr on the rings of a star,
Contemplating life from afar.
Astro-dogs fetch the moons of old,
Trading bright tales that never get cold!

Darkness giggles, sparking a game,
Polaris chuckles, 'You're all the same!'
Each twinkle holds laughter, sweet and mild,
In the vast expanse, like a playful child!

So listen close to the silence tonight,
Jokes linger softly in the starlight bright.
In the universe's heart, a mystery spins,
With each cosmic chuckle, the magic begins!

Constellations of Forgotten Lore

In the sky, the stars all yawn,
Chasing dreams until the dawn.
A turtle with a twinkling hat,
Whispers secrets to a chatty bat.

Jupiter's got a weather app,
Reports of storms that make you clap.
Mars is busy baking pies,
While Venus wears ten silly ties.

Saturn's rings are hula hoops,
Dancing with a choir of loops.
The Milky Way's a twisted slide,
Where cosmic kittens like to ride.

And in this dance of space and light,
Each star has its own delight.
With laughter echoing through the night,
In cosmic tales that feel just right.

Echoes from the Astral Sea

In the sea of stars, a fish with wings,
Sings of cosmic silly things.
A jellyfish dons a spacey crown,
While octopuses spin around town.

Asteroids chase a comet's tail,
Making bets on who will fail.
A starfish says, 'Let's do the twist!'
While aliens join in the cosmic mist.

The moon plays chess with a sandman,
While planets cheer in a funky band.
Uranus chuckles at its name,
In this galactic, silly game.

Each echo carries a wild song,
From places where the laughs belong.
So dive into this astral spree,
Where nonsense reigns in harmony.

Fragments of Galactic Reverie

A galaxy with socks mismatched,
Orbits where no pattern's hatched.
Aliens laugh at human quirks,
Trading their jokes for funny smirks.

The sun's a chef cooking light,
Stirring up joy with all its might.
Mercury's dancing on a pin,
While comets play a game to win.

Neptune's been taking a bubble bath,
Blowing soap stars with a giggly laugh.
Black holes keep losing their keys,
Swirling about with cosmic wheeze.

Fragments of mirth in every hue,
Creating whimsy just for you.
In this realm, dreams softly collide,
With winks and chuckles as our guide.

The Poetry of Cosmic Dust

Cosmic dust in a wacky swirl,
A party where space critters twirl.
Puppies on rockets zooming fast,
Shooting stars that giggle and blast.

A poetic dance of stardust trails,
Where jokes tickle like comets' tails.
Every grain plays a funny part,
In the universe's silly heart.

Planets writing notes on clouds,
Scribbled laughs that draw big crowds.
A supernova's flashy jest,
Leaving all celestial friends impressed.

Through this charming cosmic play,
We find the smiles, come what may.
And in the laughter that we trust,
We find the magic in cosmic dust.

Galaxies of Forgotten Lore

In a galaxy far, far away,
A comet once tripped on a stray sunray.
Stars giggled and twinkled, a cosmic cheer,
As planets all wobbled, 'Don't land over here!'

Asteroids dressed in their finest flair,
Danced awkwardly in spaces without a care.
While black holes whispered, 'We're not here to wait!'
Just pulling in all the clueless too late.

An alien chef cooked up grumpy stew,
While Martians argued, 'That's not how you do!'
They boiled their thoughts in a bubbling pot,
Saying, 'This is a dish that is surely not hot!'

But amidst all the chaos, tales spun like gold,
With cosmic chuckles that never grew old.
For each twinkling star had a story to share,
Of the wild, wacky wonders found everywhere.

Cosmic Mosaics

In a universe painted with colors so bright,
Planets played tag with the stars every night.
Comets would swoosh and then giggle away,
Leaving trails of stardust that glitter and play.

A giant green frog croaked the tune of the sky,
While meteors winked as they zoomed right by.
Saturn donned rings made of spaghetti and cheese,
The space chef proclaimed, 'A feast, if you please!'

Astro-kittens chased dust bunnies in space,
While rockets adorned with a bright smiley face.
Jupiter bragged with its stormy delight,
'I've got the most winds, and they really take flight!'

Yet when dusk approaches, they all come together,
For the funniest tales last through all kinds of weather.
Each star has a laugh, secrets tangled like vines,
In this cosmic mosaic where humor entwines.

Chasing Celestial Shadows

Chasing shadows through the cosmic expanse,
Stars twirled and giggled in an intergalactic dance.
Moonbeams went slip-sliding with grins on their faces,
As they hopped over comets, finding their places.

A sunbeam got tangled in a pair of old rings,
Becoming the jester who juggled bright things.
While space dust would whisper, 'Don't trip on a star!'
Because landing on Earth brings a bump or a scar!

In the corner of space, a bright purple worm,
Wiggled and jiggled, causing quite a squirm.
It traveled through time, with a wink and a jest,
'Who knew vacuum was my favorite of quests?'

The shadows all giggled, as they played hide and seek,
A swirling adventure, at the end of each week.
For in this vast cosmos, where light meets the dark,
Every tickle of starlight leaves behind a spark.

The Dance of Light and Dark

The dance of the bright against shadows so sly,
Where giggling photons twirl, aiming high.
Darkness wore sunglasses to look super cool,
While stars pulled their pranks like they were in school.

Moonlight, a ballerina, swirled with great grace,
Caught shadows off guard in a cheeky embrace.
They stomped through the cosmos in elegant shoes,
Swaying to rhythms of cosmic blues.

Black holes set up a game of charades,
While comets whipped around in shimmering parades.
They held cosmic contests, a light vs. dark fate,
Each joke would echo, 'It's never too late!'

As laughter erupted from quasars that gleamed,\nThe universe smiled, its wonders redeemed.
For every dark shadow must soon find its light,
In the dance of existence where everything's bright.

Ethereal Flights

In a realm where starfish wear hats,
And moonbeams dance on friendly bats,
Galaxies giggle, what a sight,
Comets race in joyous flight.

Asteroids roll like bowling balls,
While space cows answer cosmic calls,
Wormholes wink and create a fuss,
As lightyears pass in playful bus.

No worries here, just cosmic cheese,
Floating freely with the breeze,
Aliens trade jokes in the void,
For laughter's joy can't be destroyed.

So grab your rocket made of yarn,
Off to worlds where no one's worn,
Funny things await in sky's embrace,
Join the chase in this wild space!

Moonscapes and Daydreams

Where lunar llamas leap and trot,
On pastel hills, they've found a spot,
They sip on tea brewed from stardust,
And giggle softly with total trust.

Daydreams prance in cloudy skirts,
While shooting stars do silly flirts,
They wink at comets, who roll their eyes,
As planets spin in funny ties.

In this land of whimsical scheme,
Silly shadows playfully beam,
The sun wears shades, a quirky sight,
While rainbows dance with sheer delight.

With every laugh, the sky does twirl,
As daydreams take a graceful whirl,
Join the fun, unleash your glee,
In moonscapes bright, forever free!

The Pulse of Nebulous Realms

In realms where colors bounce and skip,
And constellations flip and dip,
The pulse of stars plays funky tunes,
While dancing meteors wear balloons.

Galactic giggles fill the air,
As friendly quarks begin to share,
Their secrets wrapped in cosmic rhyme,
In ticklish hues that twist with time.

A trampoline of laughter spans,
Bouncing dreams on cosmic plans,
While stardust spills like confetti bright,
Celebrating all through the night.

So join the beat, let merriment swell,
In nebulous realms where stories dwell,
For every pulse holds endless grin,
And every heart invites you in.

Transcendent Horizons

Where horizons stretch and flip around,
And silly shadows make no sound,
Daydreams sail on marshmallow seas,
With gummy bears dangling from trees.

Transcendent views with a twist of fate,
As wanderers dance on clouds that skate,
They shout of joy with laughter grand,
In quirky worlds, where fun is planned.

Sunshine wears a funny face,
While rainbow butterflies speed in race,
Tickling stars with laughter's cheer,
As skies embrace all who draw near.

So strap your joy with bright delight,
To horizons that banish the night,
In wondrous realms of giggles and light,
Adventure calls with pure delight!

Unraveling Celestial Mysteries

In the cosmos, where stars collide,
A lost sock wanders, a cosmic guide.
It spins and twirls in deep space's whirl,
Searching for mates in a galactic swirl.

Jupiter chuckles, "That sock's quite bold,"
While Saturn's rings whisper secrets untold.
The Milky Way giggles, a twist of fate,
As laundry day drifts into stellar debate.

A comet zooms by, with a tail so bright,
Turning in circles, it can't find the light.
"Who needs sunblock?" it shouts with glee,
A tan for my dust is the way to be free!

Galaxies dance, in a conga line,
While aliens munch on some cosmic cuisine.
"Do we have enough for this munching spree?"
"Just grab a star!" bursts out with laughter, free.

Starlit Destinies

Stars crack jokes as they twinkle bright,
"Why did the planet cross the night?"
"To get to the other side, it's true!"
"The moon's too shy, it just stays blue."

Comets throw parties, all night long,
"Bring your own ice cream, we'll sing a song!"
With confetti stardust, and laughter galore,
They dance on the rings, always wanting more.

Black holes gossip, "Did you hear that sound?"
"Just our neighbor's vacuum, it's been quite loud!"
They suck in the silence, then giggle in glee,
"Let's spin it back out, watch it float, whee!"

Planets play hide and seek in the dark,
"Pluto, you're hiding, just under a spark!"
Each twinkling body, with jokes to deliver,
In this celestial realm, we all will shiver.

Celestial Echoes

Echoes of laughter drift through the void,
As asteroids rumble, feeling overjoyed.
"Where's the buffet?" they holler and shout,
A cosmic feast that can't be without!

The sun rolls its eyes, "Oh, not this again!"
"Last time you ate all my solar zen!"
But the planets just chuckle, their humor quite bright,
"Let's gather some stardust for dinner tonight!"

Neutrinos giggle, zipping around,
"Catch us if you can, we're too fast to sound!"
They wiggle and dash like kids on the run,
While spacetime ripples, having too much fun.

Quasars twirl circles, a disco ball's spin,
"Let's turn up the light and let the dance begin!"
With cosmic confetti raining down from above,
These echoes of joy shine pure laughter and love.

Tales from the Edge of Infinity

At the edge of the cosmos, where dreams can play,
A turtle floats by, "Is this a good day?"
With stars as his friends, he sails through the night,
Inventing new games with pure delight.

"Check out my shell, it's a cosmic ride!
In zero gravity, I take pride!"
The turtles laugh hard, "Look at us spin!"
"We're lucky it's fun to just bask and grin."

Infinity beckons, with wonders untold,
As space kites flutter, in colors so bold.
"Let's soar and discover what secrets reside,
Perhaps a dance party where time tries to hide!"

A fish in the comet leaves sparkles and trails,
"Watch me swim fast, like a fairy tale!"
As all gather 'round for a wild night on high,
At the edge of forever, where giggles will fly.

Comets of Memory's Mirth

In the sky, a comet flies,
Chasing socks from laundry skies.
It spins around, a dance so bright,
Leaving trails of laughter at night.

Stars giggle in their cozy beds,
As space cats play with floating threads.
Cosmic pies that never bake,
Filling the void with every shake.

Planets party, round and round,
With balloons made of starry sound.
Aliens juggle, toasting cheer,
While black holes sip on root beer.

Galactic jokes drift through the air,
Why did the asteroid cut its hair?
To shine bright like a shooting star,
But missed and landed in a jar!

Starborn Epics in the Ether

In the ether, tales unfold,
Of space squirrels both brave and bold.
They battle meteors with a grin,
Using helmets made of tin.

Dwarf stars prank the cosmic beams,
Whispering sweet interstellar dreams.
While comets race, like kids at play,
Dodging satellites that block the way.

A galaxy wants to tell a tale,
Of how it danced with a comet's trail.
But tripped on stardust, ended down,
Rolling through the Milky Way town.

Grumpy moons roll their eyes so wide,
As giggling asteroids take a ride.
They laugh so hard, they start to spin,
And pull a prank on Pluto's grin!

The Lullaby of Distant Worlds

Hush now, starlings, close your eyes,
Dream of Mars in pink disguise.
Venus hums a gentle tune,
While Jupiter serves cosmic prunes.

Sleepy moons begin to sway,
Rocking quarks at the end of day.
Quasars blink with sleepy glee,
Singing songs of fantasy.

While Saturn spins his ring of cheer,
A tiny voice whispers, "Can't you hear?"
It's a lullaby from far and wide,
With galaxies dancing as they glide.

So drift along through astral seas,
Tickled by soft, interstellar breeze.
They giggle, bounce, and float away,
In a dream of stars that love to play.

Glimmers of Legends Beyond

Beyond the stars, legends grow,
Of a cat who stole the show.
She wore a cape made of light,
Chasing shadows into the night.

Space whales sing a silly tune,
While frolicking in a cosmic swoon.
They dive through clouds of candy dust,
Carrying dreams in stardust gust.

Ghostly comets whisper tales,
Of alien ships and flying snails.
They slip on cosmic banana peels,
While holding tight to cosmic wheels.

A galaxy's just a big game of tag,
Where each star wears a silly rag.
So giggle with the universe wide,
For laughter is the best rocket ride!

Cosmic Reverberations

In the vastness, a star sneezed,
A comet laughed, it wasn't pleased.
Galaxies juggled, so much flair,
While asteroids danced without a care.

Planets in pajamas, what a sight,
Spinning around, with all their might.
Black holes giggled, pulling with glee,
"Come here, dear Pluto, join the spree!"

Quasars winked, sending light years out,
Cheeky little photons, dancing about.
In this circus of cosmic delight,
Even the dark matter buzzed with light!

So if you gaze at the night sky high,
Remember the humor that floats by.
For in the universe, strange tales sway,
A comedy show in a vast array.

Dreams Woven in Space

Once a rocket lost its way,
It tried to nap, but aliens play!
With bubble hats and shining shoes,
They tickled the pilot, spreading the blues.

Asteroids traded jokes on the run,
"Why don't we ever have space fun?"
They zipped and zoomed, leaving trails behind,
Chasing each other, truly unconfined.

A star formed a band with a glowing flare,
"Let's rock the cosmos, nothing can compare!"
Nebula clouds swayed to the beat,
Photo-shoot selfies, no chance of defeat!

When the sun sets on dreams untold,
The universe chuckles, never gets old.
In the tapestry of sky so wide,
Laughter and light forever reside.

Skylines Beyond the Ether

On Martian rooftops, the views are grand,
With two moons overhead, it's quite unplanned.
Venusian squirrels throw space nuts around,
While Saturn's rings spin, making no sound.

Clouds on Jupiter play hide and seek,
Bouncing around, never feeling meek.
Stars have tea parties, while comets swing by,
Dashing for cookies, their sugar supply!

Constellations chit-chat, sharing their lore,
"Did you hear what Orion saw at the store?"
With laughter and joy, they twinkle with glee,
In this cosmic playground, all things agree.

So look up tonight, let your mind roam,
In the skyline of stars, we all find a home.
With quirky friends in celestial dance,
Each night unveils a new cosmic chance.

Celestial Strata

An asteroid grumbled, "I need my snack!"
While orbiting planets were on the crack.
The Milky Way giggled, swirling with grace,
As meteors raced in a hungry chase.

Supernovae twirled, sprinkling light,
In a starry fiesta that felt just right.
Time travelers wandered, wearing bright hats,
Chasing their tails, like playful cats.

Gravity pulled some, but they wouldn't stay,
"I'm having too much fun," they'd always say.
Cosmic crooners harmonized with joy,
Singing of wonders, for every girl and boy.

So marvel at space with a smile anew,
Where the tales are tangled, and laughter is true.
In celestial layers, there lies no end,
Only jokes and stories that always transcend.

Threads of Starlit Stories

Once I tangled my socks in space,
Giggles echoed in the cosmic race.
Stars fell over, laughing with glee,
Even the comets couldn't quite see.

My cat rode a rocket, what a sight!
Chasing the moon with all of her might.
She swore she met aliens long ago,
They traded purrs for a cosmic glow.

When I tried to dance on Saturn's rings,
I found out gravity's tricky little things.
Bouncing around like a playful flea,
I landed on Jupiter—oh, woe is me!

In a galaxy far, with ice-cream stars,
We wrote our tales on Mars with guitars.
The sun held a concert, and laughter soared,
In the universe's party, never ignored.

Eclipsed by Infinity

A sun so shy, it wore a hat,
Hiding behind clouds, began to chat.
The moon declared, 'Let's play peek-a-boo!'
That's how eclipses got their debut.

An alien danced with two left feet,
Slipped on some stardust, oh what a feat!
Giggles erupted from planets all round,
As they rolled on their axes, cosmic sound.

The black hole yawned, it sucked in a star,
Belched out some comets, what a bizarre!
We laughed as the universe spun in circles,
Creating chaos with its endless swirls.

In this vastness, the pranks never cease,
With every new twinkle, the laughter's a beast.
Time winks at us with a goofy grin,
In the cosmic jester's game, we all win.

Celestial Legends in the Void

A skunk in space, how strange it seemed,\nHe banished
the silence, while others dreamed.
Floating away on a cloud of cheese,
All the stars conspired to sneeze!

The astronaut ducks wear medals of gold,
For daring exploits, so brash and bold.
One even raced with a shooting star,
And claimed twelve cookies from the cosmic bar.

In an infinite library, books stacked high,
Stories of fish that learned how to fly.
The librarian's a starfish, oh what a twist,
Who shushed the comets when they laughed in the mist.

Jupiter's storms have slapstick delight,
They tickle the moons, such a silly sight.
Through the universe, these tales will unfurl,
As laughter courses and dreams start to swirl.

Astral Journeys of the Heart

A heart-shaped star flew past my eye,
Winking at Venus, oh me, oh my!
They giggled and twirled in a cosmic ball,
While planets in orbit began to sprawl.

We rode on beams with a bubble of light,
Sailing through shadows, oh what a flight!
Even the meteors joined the cheer,
Showering laughter as we drew near.

An asteroid rock band started to play,
Melodies echoed through the Milky Way.
With riffs so stellar, the echoes grew,
With a punchline or two we just had to spew!

Across the cosmos, friendships grew wide,
Stars hold our secrets like whispers inside.
In this fun universe where stories impart,
Every giggle's a treasure—a journey of heart!

www.ingramcontent.com/pod-product-compliance
Lightning Source LLC
Chambersburg PA
CBHW070750220426
43209CB00083B/395